Advanced English Synonyms

Improve English Speaking

By Mohit Joshi

Copyright Notice

Please Note That The Content In This Guide Is Protected Under Copyright Law. This Guide Is For Your Personal Use Only. No Part Of This Guide May Be Reproduced, Stored In A Retrieval System, Or Transmitted, In Any Form Or By Any Means, Electronic, Mechanical, Recording, Or Otherwise, Without The Prior Written Permission Of The Author.

Copy Right Holder – Mohit Joshi
License – Standard Copyright License
Year of Publication – 2013

Table of Content

Advanced English Synonyms 1
Copyright Notice.. 2
ENGLISH SYNONYMS 4
MORE SYNONYMS 9
About The Author 38

ENGLISH SYNONYMS

("sb" implies somebody, "sth" implies something)

arduous / strenuous involving a lot of effort and energy

assiduous / diligent / sedulous showing care and effort in your work or duties

fastidious / meticulous / scrupulous giving careful attention to every detail

ebullient / effervescent / exuberant / rollicking full of energy, excitement, etc.

dejected / despondent / disconsolate unhappy and disappointed

discomfit / disconcert / faze to make sb feel confused or embarrassed

****

SYNONYMS FOR "TO MAKE SOMEBODY VERY ANGRY"

antagonize / enrage / exasperate / infuriate / incense / raise sb's hackles to make sb very angry

****

SYNONYMS FOR "ANNOYED"

brassed off / crooked on sb / cross with sb / disgruntled / fed up / hacked off / miffed / narked / peeved   annoyed

pique   annoyed because your pride has been hurt

get under sb's skin   to annoy sb

grate on sb / irk   to annoy sb

vex   to annoy or worry sb

vexatious   making you feel annoyed or worried

****

SYNONYMS FOR "TO AVOID"

dodge / elude / eschew / evade / fight shy of sth / fudge / gloss over / skirt around sth / skate over sth / shun / shy away from sth   to avoid

****

SYNONYMS FOR "BAD-TEMPERED"

cantankerous / choleric / crotchety / crusty / dyspeptic / grumpy / irritable / peevish / petulant / ratty / splenetic / sourpuss / stroppy / tetchy   bad-tempered

****

SYNONYMS FOR "TO CRITICIZE"

castigate / censure / chastise / deplore / denounce / excoriate / flay / fulminate / inveigh against sb/sth / lampoon / lash out at sb / pan / pillory / pull sb up / rap / revile / upbraid   to criticize

get / give a rap over the knuckle   to get / give criticism

hit out at sb/sth   to criticize

pounce on   to quickly criticize

second guess   to guess, to criticize

slam   to bang, to criticize

slate   to plan that sth will happen at a particular time in future, to criticize

take a swipe at sb / take sb to task   to criticize

****

SYNONYMS FOR "HAPPINESS"

elation   great happiness, excitement

exultation   great pride or happiness

bliss / ecstasy / felicity / jubilation / joie de vivre   great happiness

****

SYNONYMS FOR "NONSENSE"

balderdash / bunkum / flimflam / gibberish / guff / hogwash / mumbo-jumbo / piffle / poppy-cock / tommyrot / tosh / twaddle nonsense

****

SYNONYMS FOR "STUPID PERSON"

berk / charlie / chump / duffer / / imbecile / jackass / jerk / lamebrain / nincompoop / pillock / putz / prat / plonker / wally stupid person

****

SYNONYMS FOR "TO SUPPORT"

champion / endorse / espouse / second / uphold / underpin to support

countenance person's face or expression, to support

corroborate to confirm, to support

****

SYNONYMS FOR "VERY TIRED"

dead beat / be done in / fagged out / haggard / knackered / pooped out / zonked out   very tired

****

MORE SYNONYMS

abhor / loathe to dislike sb/sth very much

ablaze / aflame on fire

abnegation / abstinence / renunciation the act of rejecting food, alcoholic drinks, intercourse, etc.

adamant / intransigent / obdurate / obstinate stubborn

accentuate / hammer home / underline / underscore to emphasize

accord / impart to give

accordingly / ergo therefore

accreditation / imprimatur official approval

adage / dictum saying

adduce / moot / propound to propose, to put forward

adept / adroit skilful

adherent / cohort / proponent supporter

adolescence / puberty time in a person's life when he or she develops from a child into an adult

adversary / antagonist opponent

adversity / bummer unpleasant situation

under the aegis of sb/sth / under the auspices of sb/sth with the protection or support of sb/sth

aerobics / calisthenics / work-out physical exercise

affable / amiable / genial / jovial pleasant, friendly   **amicable** polite or friendly

affray / brawl fight or violent behaviour in a public place

afresh / anew again

agile / nimble able to move quickly and easily

agitation / angst / nerves feelings of anxiety, worry

agony / anguish / torment severe physical or mental suffering

agony aunt / agony uncle / advice columnist who gives answers to readers' questions in a newspaper or magazine

aisle / gangway passage between rows of seats of theatre, aircraft, etc.

all in good time / in due course at the right time and not before

allay / alleviate / appease / assuage / mitigate to make less severe

alleluia / hallelujah song or shout of praise to god

alluring smile / engaging smile attractive smile

aloof / recluse / standoffish not interested in other people

antediluvian / antiquated / archaic old fashioned

apprehension / foreboding / premonition / presentiment / trepidation anxiety, fear

apprise / notify to inform

argot / lingo / jargon / parlance   words or language related to particular subject or field

armoury / arsenal   place where weapons and armour are kept

asinine / feather-brained / gormless / tomfool   stupid

asphyxiate / stifle / suffocate   to feel difficulty in taking breathe

assail / assault   to attack sb violently

assert / aver   to state firmly

assignation / tryst   secret meeting with a lover

astute / canny / shrewd   clever, intelligent, careful

attribute / impute   to say, sb is responsible for sth or has a particular quality

attuned to sth / conversant with sth   familiar with sth

audacity / temerity   boldness

auspicious / propitious / promising   showing signs of being good or successful

autocrat / despot   ruler who has complete power

avarice / cupidity   greed

axe / sack   to dismiss sb from job

backbiting / backstabbing   unpleasant talk about sb who is not present

backhander / kickback   bribe

badger / importune / pester to annoy sb by asking sth many times

badinage / banter friendly joking between people

bairn / nipper / rug rat child

barrage / fusillade continuous and rapid firing

bawdy / lewd / lubricious / salacious / scabrous / smutty obscene

catch sb off balance / throw sb off balance to make sb/sth unsteady and in danger of falling

backfire (on sb) / boomerang (on sb) to have bad or dangerous effect on sb

bald-faced / barefaced / blatant making no attempt to hide your dishonest behaviour

balk / baulk to be unwilling

bank on sb/sth / count on sb/sth / lean on sb/sth to rely, to depend

barbarous / barbaric / vicious cruel and violent

barf / puke / throw up to vomit

barrack / heckle to shout criticism

bash away at sth / bash on sth / plug away at sth to work hard at sth

be at odds with sth / go against the grain different from sth

bear all / in the buff naked

beastly / odious   horrible

bedevil / beset   to be surrounded by problems

bedspread / counterpane   bed-cover

behead / decapitate   to cut off sb's head

belch / burp   to let air come up noisily from stomach and out through the mouth

belittle / denigrate / disparage   to make sb or the things that sb does seem unimportant

bellicose / belligerent / pugnacious   aggressive

bellboy / bellhop   whose job is to carry people's cases to their rooms in a hotel

belly button / tummy button   navel

bench-mark / touchstone   point of reference

beneficent / munificent / benevolent   generous

beseech / entreat / implore   to beg

bewitch / enchant / enrapture   to attract or impress sb very much

bibulous / dipsomaniac / drunkard   alcoholic

big bucks / riches   large amount of money

bird watcher / ornithologist   person, who studies birds

bizarre / uncanny / weird   strange, eerie

black out / pass out   to faint

blatant / flagrant shameless

bloodbath / carnage / massacre / pogrom killing of a lot of people

bloodletting / bloodshed killing or wounding of people

bogus / counterfeit / phoney fake

bolster / buttress to strengthen

booklet / leaflet / pamphlet small thin book

boon companion / bosom friend very good friend

bootlicker / flunkey / sycophant / toady who praises important or powerful person too much to get sth from them

botch / bungle / flub / cock up / mess up / screw up to spoil

brat / perisher / tyke child, who behaves badly

brawny / burly (of a man) big, strong and heavy

Bristol fashion / ship shape in good order; neat and clean

brood / mope to think too much and sadly about sth

bulge / protuberance a lump sticking out from sth in a round shape

bustle / crinoline a frame worn under a skirt by women to hold the skirt out at the back

busybody / nosy parker too interested in other people's affairs

bystander / on-looker who watches sth happening without involving in it

cabriolet / convertible a car with a roof that can be folded down or removed

cadence / intonation / lilt rise and fall of the voice in speaking

cagey / evasive secretive

cajole / coax to persuade sb gently

calamity / catastrophe disaster

call a spade a spade / speak your mind to say exactly what you think

calumny / malign / slander / traduce to say unpleasant things about sb

canyon / gorge / gulch / ravine deep and narrow valley with steep sides

capacious / commodious / spacious roomy

caper / frolic / frisk / gambol / romp to jump in excited way

caprice / whim sudden wish

captivate / fascinate / mesmerize to attract or interest sb very much

careen / career / hurtle of a person or vehicle, to move in dangerous way

caress / fondle to touch sb sexually or affectionately

cast-off / hand-me-down piece of clothing no longer worn by the original owner

cachet / kudos respect and admiration

celebrity / legendary very famous person, fame

cerumen / earwax wax-like substance produced in the ear

chalk up / notch up to achieve

chap / bloke / blighter man

chary / leery / wary cautious

cheap-stake / scrooge / stingy / tightfisted who avoids spending money, etc.

chime in with sth / chip in with sth to join or interrupt a conversation

chiropodist / podiatrist doctor of the ailments of feet

chuck / lob / hurl / sling to throw

chum / pal friend

circuitous / roundabout of a route or journey, long and not direct

clam up on sb / send sb to Coventry to refuse to speak to sb

clamber / scramble to climb with difficulty using hands and feet

colloquy / confabulation conversation

collywobbles / the heebie-jeebies feeling of nervous fear and worry

chance upon sb/sth / come across sb/sth / stumble across/upon/on sb/sth to discover sb/sth unexpectedly

commendable / laudable deserving to be praised

commiserate with sb / empathize to show sympathy

commiseration / empathy sympathy

compère / emcee who introduces performers in a show

complacent / smug satisfied

complicity / collusion act of taking part in a crime

comply / conform to obey

conciliate / mollify / pacify / placate / propitiate to calm sb

concurrence / consonance / tie-up agreement

condescend to do sth / deign to do sth to do sth that shows as if your are too important to do it

confab / symposium meeting or conference

conflagration / inferno large fire

confute / controvert / rebut / refute to prove sth wrong, to deny

conjecture / surmise to guess

conjugal / connubial related to marriage or husband-wife

consequence / import importance

consort with sb / hobnob with sb / hook up with sb / rub shoulder with sb to spend time with sb

convalesce / recuperate to spend time gaining your health back after an illness

convene / convoke to come together for a formal meeting:

cookie / hombre   man of particular type

cornice / moulding   decorated border around the top of the wall

contravene / infringe   to break a law or rule

cove / dude   man

cower / cringe   to crouch and/or move backwards because of fear

crouch / hunker down / squat   to sit on your heels with your knees bent up in front of you

crackdown / clamp down   severe measures to restrict criminal people, or actions

cram for sth / swot for sth   to learn quickly in a short period, for an exam

cramps / griping pain   severe stomach pain

cream puff / wimp   weak or frightened

creep / sidle / skulk / slink   to move quietly so that no one can see you

creepy / spooky   strange and frightening

cull / slay   to kill

cut loose / let loose   to do sth or happen in uncontrolled way

dandy / fop   man who cares a lot about his clothes and the way he looks

dash / rush   to go somewhere quickly

dawdle / dilly-dally   to take a long time to do sth or go somewhere

dither / shilly-shally   to take a long time to do sth or to make a decision

deadlock / impasse / stalemate / standoff   situation in which no agreement can be reached

dearth / paucity / scarcity   shortage

decorum / propriety   polite behaviour appropriate in a social situation

decree / edict / fiat   official order that becomes the law

defer / mothball / put off   to postpone

defray costs / defray expenses / pay up / settle up   to pay the money

degenerate / deteriorate   to become worse

delectable / scrummy / scrumptious / yummy   delicious

delectation / glee   delight

deplorable / reprehensible   morally wrong and deserving criticism

derision / disdain / scorn   the feeling that sb/sth does not deserve your respect or attention

derogatory / pejorative   insulting

despoil / pillage   to plunder

deter / foil / preclude / scupper / stymie / thwart   to prevent

dialect / patois / vernacular   local language

dilapidated / ramshackle / tumbledown in very bad condition

dilemma / predicament / quandary problem

diminutive / Lilliputian very small

discord / dissension disagreement

disembowel / eviscerate to remove the inner organs of a body

dishevelled / unkempt of hair, clothes, appearance, very untidy

dismal / dour gloomy

dissolute / rakish / reprobate who enjoys immoral activities

distraught / over-wrought upset and anxious

dodgy / fishy suspicious

dogsbody / gofer who does small jobs for people in a company

domineering / highhanded / overbearing trying to control other people without considering their opinions or feelings

dormant / quiescent inactive

downplay / soft-pedal to take sth lightly

downpour / rain-storm / torrential rain heavy rain

drenched / soaked / sodden / soaking / sopping very wet

dress up / gussy up to dress yourself in attractive way

dust-up / face-off / fracas fight or argument

eccentricity / idiosyncrasy a person's unusual way of behaving, thinking, etc.

ecstatic / rapturous enthusiastic

eddy / maelstrom / whirl-pool vortex

effrontery / nerve confident, rude, shameless behaviour

egg on sb / incentivize to encourage

ejaculate / exclaim to say sth suddenly and loudly

elucidate / explicate / expound to explain

emaciated / weedy thin, weak

embalm / mummify to prevent a dead body from decaying by using special substances

embitter / rankle to make sb feel angry or upset over long period of time

embodiment / epitome a typical example of an idea or a quality

eminence / renown fame and respect

eminent / renowned famous and respected

encapsulate / recapitulate / sum up to summarize

encomium / eulogy / panegyric speech or writing praising sb/sth

enthralling / spell binding holding your attention completely

entourage / retinue people who travel with an important person

entrance / enthrall / engross (of sb/sth) to give great pleasure to sb, that they give all time, attention to them

enthralling / spellbinding very interesting

exchange vows / go/walk down the aisle / tie a knot / get hitched to get married

excrement / faeces / poo / poop   solid waste passed from the body

excursion / jaunt / outing   short journey for pleasure

Ex-flame / old flame   former lover

expletive / imprecation   swear word

extempore / impromptu   spoken or done without any previous preparation

extol / eulogize   to praise

facetious / flippant   joking

facile / glib   using words that are clever and quick, but not sincere

facsimile / replica   exact copy of sth

fanatic / maniac / zealot   enthusiast, extremist

fanlight / transom   window above the door

faux pas / gaffe   action or a remark that causes embarrassment because it is not socially correct

fawn (on sb) / ingratiate yourself (with sb)   to try to please sb very much

fess up / own up   to confess

fetid / musty / smelly / stinky / stinking   having bad smell

fetish / fixation / obsession / preoccupation   state of a person's mind being completely filled with the thoughts of sb/sth

fetter / manacle / shackle   to tie sb with chains

filch / pinch   to steal

fink / toad   unpleasant person

fit sb/sth in / squeeze sb/sth in   to give time to sb although you are busy

fizzle out / peter out   to end completely but slowly

fleeting / transitory   brief

flourish / thrive   to grow or develop quickly

fly-by / fly-over / fly-past   air show

fool around / goof around / mess around   to waste time

foresee / foretell   to predict

fork out / shell out   to spend a lot of money

forthwith / out of hand / pronto / right away / right off / right now / without (more) ado   immediately

freakish / freak   unusual

fulcrum / kernel   most important part of sth

gabble / gibber / jabber   to speak very quickly

gaffer / honcho   boss

galling / incendiary / inflammatory / offending   making you angry

gangling / lanky   tall, thin, awkward in movements

gargantuan / gigantic / ginormous   extremely large

garish / gaudy   brightly coloured in unpleasant way

garner / muster / summon   to gather

garrulous / loquacious   talkative

gathering / get-together   meeting

gazillion / squillion / zillion   very large number

gear up for sth / gird up for sth   to prepare for sth

geek / nerd   boring, stupid and not fashionable; very interested in computer

get along/on with sb / hit it off with sb   to have a friendly relationship with sb

ghastly / grisly   causing horror

gingerly / studiously   carefully

git / oaf   stupid, unpleasant man

glare / glower   to look in angry, aggressive way

glassy eyes / glazed eyes   showing no emotion

glister / glitter   to shine like diamond; to sparkle

go ballistic / hit the roof / fume   to become very angry

go off at half cock / jump the gun   to do sth, before the right time

gorge yourself / stuff yourself   to eat too much food

grandiloquent / pompous / pretentious using long or complicated words to impress people

grandeur / splendor the quality of being great and impressive in appearance

grasping / rapacious greedy

gratuitous / otiose / redundant / superfluous / uncalled-for unnecessary

gravid / preggers pregnant

greenhorn / tenderfoot who has little experience and can be easily tricked

grind / swot a person who studies too much

gripe / grouse / grumble to complain

grudge / rancour feeling of anger or hatred towards sb because of sth bad done to you by them

guzzle / quaff to drink sth quickly and in large amounts

habituated to sth / wont to do sth accustomed

hammered / inebriated / pie-eyed / pissed / plastered / sloshed / smashed / sozzled / tanked / tanked up drunk

harass / harry / hassle / hound to annoy or worry sb

harp on / prattle on / ramble on to talk a lot

have your back to the walls / be up a gum tree to be in a difficult situation

headstone / gravestone / tombstone stone placed at one end of a grave, showing the name, etc. of the person buried there

hex / sorcery black magic

high-rise building / skyscraper very tall building in a city

hinder / hamper to make it difficult for sb to do sth or sth to happen

hooker / harlot / strumpet / whore prostitute

horrendous / horrid / horrific horrible, frightening

hothead / impetuous who always does things in a hurry and without thinking carefully

ménage / household all the people living in one house

humiliate / mortify to make sb feel ashamed or stupid and lose the respect of other people

humongous / humungous / immense enormous

hunk / husky big, strong and sexually attractive man

immanent / prevalent / rife / rampant common, widespread

imminent / impending about to happen very soon

immoderate / unconscionable / undue excessive

in a bind / in a fix / in the soup in a difficult situation

in shreds / in tatters very badly damaged

inappropriate / incongruous not suitable in a particular situation

incarcerate / intern to put sb in prison

incentive / inducement encouragement

inchoate / incipient just beginning

incriminate / implicate to show that sb is involved in a crime

inculcate sth into sb / instill sth into sb to fill sth into sb

intermittent / spasmodic / sporadic happening at irregular intervals

insouciance / nonchalance calm and relaxed behaviour

insurrection / sedition / uprising / rebellion use of words or actions against an established government

itsy-bitsy / itty-bitty very small

jaunty / jocund / jolly cheerful

jazz up / juice up to make sth more interesting, exciting

josh / raze to tease

jumble sale / rummage sale a sale of used or old clothes, etc.

fend sb/sth off / ward sb/sth off to protect or defend yourself against sb/sth

keepsake / memento / memorabilia / souvenir a thing that reminds you of sb/sth

kip / slumber sleep, to sleep

kowtow to sb / suck up to sb   to show sb in authority too much respect

jerk / jolt   to move or to make sth move with a sudden short sharp movement

jut / protrude   to stick out from a place or a surface

lackey / minion   servant

laconic / taciturn   using a few words to say sth

larder / pantry   cupboard or small room for storing food

lately / of late   recently

latitude / leeway   freedom

lavatory / loo   toilet or bathroom

laxative / purgative   a medicine, etc. that causes bowels to empty

lay sth bare / let slip sth   to tell the secrets

lecherous / libertine / licentious lecher type   **lecher**   obsessive for sex

leaf (through) sth / riffle (through) sth   to turn over papers or the pages of a book quickly

lousy with sth / fraught with sth / overrun with sth   filled with sth

lout / punk / yob   who behaves in a rude and aggressive way

Lucifer / Satan   devil

lukewarm / tepid   slightly warm

lusty / robust healthy and strong

make up with sb / make it up to become friends again

mandatory / obligatory compulsory

manipulate / manoeuvre / ploy to control or influence a situation in a skilful but sometimes dishonest way

maroon / strand to leave sb in a place from which they have no way of leaving

maudlin / mawkish / mushy / soppy sentimental

maven / versed expert

maxim / proverb well-known phrase

meagre / measly / paltry small in quantity and poor in quality

mess / shambles dirty, or untidy state

minus / sans without

mire / quagmire / morass bog

mob / rabble / throng crowd of people

modest / self-effacing / unassuming not wanting to draw attention to yourself

modicum / soupcon / a tad very small amount

modish / trendy fashionable

mortician / undertaker whose job is to prepare the bodies of dead people to be buried or cremated

muggy / sultry of weather, warm and damp in an unpleasant way

mumble / mutter to speak or say sth in a quiet voice

mundane / prosaic dull, ordinary

mushroom / proliferate / snowball to increase rapidly

nauseous / queasy feeling as if you want to vomit

nose-gay / posy small bunch of flowers

nosy / inquisitive curious, enquiring

notable / personage famous or important person

novice / rookie / tyro who is new and has little experience of sth

nowt / zilch nothing

one-off / one-shot happening only once

onerous / taxing requiring much effort; causing worry or problem

orotund / stentorian (of a voice) loud and powerful

other than / barring except

out-cast / pariah who is not acceptable to society

outflank / outmaneuver to gain advantage over sb by doing sth unexpected

outfox / outsmart / outwit to gain an advantage over sb by being more clever than they are

outmoded / passé no longer fashionable or useful

outrageous / preposterous shocking and unacceptable

outskirt / suburbs area far away from the centre of a city

over and over again / over and over / time and time again / time and again often

overweening / supercilious / uppity arrogant

pallid / pasty / sallow pale and not healthy

panorama / vista beautiful view

par excellence / peerless better than all others of its kind

parley / powwow meeting

parlous / perilous dangerous

patrimony / legacy inheritance

pedestal / plinth block of stone on which a column or statue stands

pelmet / valance strip of wood or cloth to hide curtail rail

penitent / repentant / remorseful feeling very sorry for doing sth wrong or bad

perceptive / pronounced noticeable

perfidious / treacherous dangerous, deceitful

betrayal / perfidy / treachery disloyalty

perish / pop your clogs / pop off to die

perspicacious / percipient / perceptive able to understand sb/sth quickly and accurately

piddling / piffling small and unimportant, trivial

pigeon hole / shelve to postpone, to abandon

placenta / the after birth material coming out of a woman body after the birth of a child

play hooky / play truant to stay away from school without leave

platter / salver large plate to serve food, drink

plebiscite / referendum a vote by people of a country or region on a particular issue

plimsoll / sneaker / trainer a sport shoe

plod / traipse / trudge to walk slowly with heavy steps

plonk / plunk to put sth down noisily

podium / rostrum / soapbox a small raised platform for a person to stand on to make a speech

post natal / post partum after the birth of a child

precursor to sth / prelude to sth that comes or happens before sth more important

prep / prime to prepare

prig / prim / prissy / prude too careful to always behave correctly and easily shocked by rude behaviour, etc.

primeval / primal / primordial connected with the earliest period of the history

pristine / immaculate perfectly clean and tidy

proceeds / spoils   profits

proclivity / propensity   tendency to a particular kind of behaviour

procrastinate / stave off   to delay sth

prodigal / profligate   extravagant

prudish / strait-laced   having strict moral attitude

psycho / psychopath / sociopath   mentally ill and behaves in violent way

pucker up / ruck up   of clothes, etc. to form untidy folds

put the kibosh on sth / put the mocker on sth   to stop sth from happening

qualm / misgiving / reservation   doubt or anxiety

quell / scotch / stem   to stop

ramp up / shore up   to increase

rat-tat / pit-a-pat   sound of knocking on a door

rattle off / reel off / regurgitate   to say sth from memory without having to think very hard

have recourse to sth / resort to sth   to use sth as a only possible solution in difficult situation

red blooded / virile   strong and full of sexual energy

reek of sth / stink of sth   to smell strongly

rejoinder / riposte   quick reply

relinquish / renounce to abandon

relish / savour to enjoy

repartee / swordplay clever and amusing comments and replies made quickly

reprisal / retaliation / vendetta / vengeance revenge

repudiate / spurn to reject, to deny

rescind / revoke to officially cancel sth

resolute / resolved determined

resurrect / resuscitate to revive

reticent / unforthcoming unwilling to tell people about things

ribald / saucy referring to sex in a rude but humorous way

ride on sth / turn on sth to depend on sth

roll sb over / lick / shellac / whup to defeat sb easily

rout / trounce to defeat sb heavily

rota / roster a list of jobs and the people who have to do them in turn

rotund / roly-poly / stocky / stout / tubby / plump small and round

rubicund / ruddy of a person's face, very red

ruckus / rumpus commotion

ruffle / rumple to disturb the smooth surface of sth   **she ruffled his hair**

sagacious / sage wise

scalawag / scallywag / scamp   child who behaves badly

scalper / tout / ticket tout   who buys tickets for concerts, etc. and then sells at a higher price

scraggy / scrawny   thin and not healthy

scrawl / scribble   to write quickly and carelessly

scuffle / tussle   short struggle

secluded / solitary   alone, single

seclusion / solitude   state of being alone

seductive / slinky   sexually attractive, enticing

seer / soothsayer   who can predict future

serene / tranquil   calm and peaceful

simmer (with sth) / seethe   to be filled with anger etc.

sinewy / wiry   (of a person) thin but strong

sip / sup   to drink sth, especially in small amounts

sissy / wimp   only interested in the sort of things girls like

slaughter house / abattoir   where animals are killed for food

sleep over / slumber party   to pass night in the same house

slew / swerve / veer   of a vehicle, to turn direction suddenly

smashing / swell   very good, enjoyable

sordid / squalid   dirty and unpleasant; immoral or dishonest

splurge / squander   to waste money

splutter / sputter explosive sound, spitting sound

stagger / totter to walk or move with weak unsteady steps

staggering / stupendous astounding

stalwart / staunch faithful

stammer / stutter to have difficulty in speaking

stern / stringent strict

stinker / unenviable unpleasant or difficult

strangle / throttle to kill sb by squeezing their throat and neck

subvert / undermine to make weaker

sulk / sulky / sullen to be in anger and not to talk

superb / stellar / terrific excellent

supervene / transpire to happen

take stock of sth / ponder to consider

tarnish / taint to spoil the good opinion people have of sb/sth

teeny / weeny / teeny-weeny tiny

tell off / tick off to scold sb

thence-forth / there-upon after that

throw a hissy fit / throw a tantrum to behave angrily and unreasonably

thumping / whopping very big

tinge / tint small amount of colour

top-flight / top-notch   of highest quality

topple / tumble   to fall

triad / trinity   group of three

twerp / twit   stupid or annoying person

unbecoming / unflattering   not suiting a particular person

he is under cloud / he is under scanner   he may have done sth wrong

upright / upstanding / virtuous   behaving in a moral and honest way

verbalize / vocalize   to express in words

vociferous / voluble / tumultuous   very loud

welfare / well-being   general health, happiness

with hindsight / in retrospect   if we now think about the past

zest / zing   zeal

****

About The Author

Mohit Joshi, The Author Of This Book Is Graduate In 'Electronics And Communication Engineering' & Is GATE (Graduate Aptitude Test In Engineering) Qualified. He Is Particularly Interested In Cosmology & High Energy Physics. Albert Einstein & Richard Feynman Are His Favourite Nobel Laureates. Tennis Is His Favourite Sport. **MohitJoshi.com** Is the Personal Website of The Author.

Connect with Mohit
Amazon Author Page:
https://www.amazon.com/author/mohitjoshi

****

Printed in Great Britain
by Amazon.co.uk, Ltd.,
Marston Gate.